How To...
Build Guitar Chops

By Chad Johnson

ISBN 978-1-4950-2736-9

HAL•LEONARD®

7777 W. BLUEMOUND RD. P.O. BOX 13819 MILWAUKEE, WI 53213

In Australia Contact:
Hal Leonard Australia Pty. Ltd.
4 Lentara Court
Cheltenham, Victoria, 3192 Australia
Email: ausadmin@halleonard.com.au

Visit Hal Leonard Online at
www.halleonard.com

CONTENTS

Page

3   ABOUT THE AUTHOR

3   DEDICATION AND ACKNOWLEDGMENTS

4   INTRODUCTION

4   HOW TO USE THIS BOOK

9   ABOUT THE AUDIO

9   WARMUP EXERCISES

10   CHAPTER 1
ALTERNATE PICKING, PART 1 – EVEN GROUPINGS

22   CHAPTER 2
ALTERNATE PICKING, PART 2 – ODD AND MIXED GROUPINGS

30   CHAPTER 3
ECONOMY AND SWEEP PICKING

40   CHAPTER 4
LEGATO

47   AFTERWORD

48   APPENDIX

ABOUT THE AUTHOR

Chad Johnson is a freelance author, editor, and musician. For Hal Leonard Corporation, he's authored over 70 instructional books covering a variety of instruments and topics, including *Guitarist's Guide to Scales Over Chords*, *How to Fingerpick Songs on Guitar*, *How to Record at Home on a Budget*, *Teach Yourself to Play Bass Guitar*, *Ukulele Aerobics*, *Pentatonic Scales for Guitar*, *Pink Floyd Guitar Signature Licks*, and *Play Like Robben Ford*, to name but a few. He's a featured guitar instructor on the DVD *200 Country Licks* (also published by Hal Leonard) and has toured and performed throughout the East Coast in various bands, sharing the stage with members of Lynyrd Skynyrd, the Allman Brothers Band, Jamey Johnson, and others. He works as a session instrumentalist, composer/songwriter, and recording engineer when not authoring or editing and also enjoys tinkering with electronics. Chad currently resides in Denton, Texas (north Dallas) with his wife and two children. Feel free to contact him at *chadjohnsonguitar@gmail.com* with any questions or concerns; you can also connect with him at *www.facebook.com/chadjohnsonguitar* to hear about his latest book releases and other musical adventures.

DEDICATION AND ACKNOWLEDGMENTS

I'd like to dedicate this book to my lovely family: my wife, Alli, my son, Lennon, and my daughter, Leherie. I'd also like to dedicate it to my parents, Mike and Kay, and my sister Mika for their continued support throughout the years. They had to endure a lot of ugly guitar noises emanating from my room during my formative years. (Now, of course, they can't hear those ugly noises anymore; I moved out long ago.)

Thanks much to the staff at Hal Leonard Corporation for their hard work and dedication to putting out such high-quality products.

INTRODUCTION

Welcome to *How to Build Guitar Chops*. If there's one thing that practically all guitarists have experienced at one time or another, it's the disappointment that comes from not being able to play something we want. Whether copping a lick from a song, learning an entire solo note for note, or trying to bring to life our own musical ideas, if your chops aren't up to it, it can prove quite disappointing. This is nothing new, of course, and there's only one way through it (deals with the devil notwithstanding)— practice, practice, practice! The only problem is that sometimes it's difficult to know exactly *what* to practice. That's where this book comes in.

In order to know what to practice, you first need to decide which skills need improvement. This book assumes that you want to improve your technical facility on the electric guitar. Though the book will cater most specifically to the broad spectrum of rock guitar, the techniques can, of course, be applied to a myriad of styles. Every book needs a focus, however. Suffice it to say that, if you want to learn how to blow fluently over ii–V–I jazz progressions in every key, you should look elsewhere. But if you want to improve your speed and accuracy on the electric guitar, you're in the right place.

There are certainly many technique books written for guitar, creating a vast resource for players who are patient and willing to put in the time, but there's a common theme among many of these: very non-musical exercises. Written with the real-world player in mind, *How to Build Guitar Chops* seeks to prove that technique can actually be fun and musical. Let's face it: The average guitarist can only take so many chromatic exercises before his or her head explodes.

In this book, with the exception of a few "1–2–3–4"-type warmup exercises, every effort has been made to make the examples musical and interesting—while still managing to isolate specific techniques. The benefit from this is twofold: First, it helps prevent boredom; there are few things as insipid as running the same chromatic lick up and down the fretboard ad infinitum. Second, it will most likely aid in your overall musicianship. Whereas mind-numbing finger gymnastics won't do much to improve your melodic abilities, exercises of a more musical nature will help to expand your vocabulary and train your ear. You may even find yourself sneaking some of these licks into your own playing!

So, without further ado, let's get on with the proceedings. We have a lot of ground to cover on your road to technical freedom!

HOW TO USE THIS BOOK

For some reason, many guitarists seem to think that a disciplined, slow-and-steady approach shouldn't apply; we tend to often want immediate gratification. This can lead to mistakes—a lot of them.

Mistakes lead to frustration, and frustration can cause some players to quit altogether. At the very least, it often makes people fall back on things that they already know, which also prevents growth. Remember: If you could play anything you wanted, at the speed you wanted, on the first try, you wouldn't need this book!

Necessary Tools

Before we get down to business, let's talk about a few things you'll need along your journey. For our purposes, this includes:

- **An electric guitar that's set up well and ready to play:** You don't want your guitar fighting you along the way, so, if you're not knowledgeable on the subject, spending $50 or so to get a professional setup is well worth the money. If you've never had it done before, the difference will likely be night and day. Your guitar will play more in tune throughout, the string tension will feel better, and the action will be optimally set.

- **A metronome:** Don't even *think* about starting this book without one! I'm serious about this; I will hunt you down! You can probably find a free app for your phone (or spend a dollar or two), or you can purchase a hardware version for less than $10. If you have a tuner, check to see if it includes a metronome, as many do.

- **A method for recording yourself:** This could be a fancy setup, such as an audio interface paired with a DAW (digital audio workstation) on your computer or a standalone digital recorder, or it could simply be the voice recorder on your smartphone. Even that dusty old tape recorder from your parent's closet will work—as long as it plays at the correct speed!

- **A notebook or journal:** It's very helpful to make notes on your progress, detailing any revelations you have, problem areas that need your attention, or goals you'd like to achieve.

- **Music notation/tab paper:** This is helpful for jotting down ideas you may get while practicing or for transcribing licks or solos from your favorite recordings (it doesn't always have to be guitar, either!). It's not uncommon at all for an exercise to inspire an altogether new idea.

Meet Mr. Metronome

Say hello to my little friend: Mr. Metronome. Without question, it's one of the most valuable tools we have at our disposal when working on technique. Not only does a metronome make clear our tendencies to rush or drag when playing, it also provides benchmarks with which to measure our progress. Be warned: If you don't have much experience playing with a metronome (or drum machine, etc.), the results can be quite shocking the first time. And the first time you record yourself playing along with a metronome is usually even more so.

Far and away, most players have a tendency to rush when playing along with a click. I'm sure there's a psychological reason for this, but I don't know what it is. All I know is that it was my tendency, and the same goes for just about every other person I've known throughout my music career. That little tick-tick-ticking is a cold, callous S.O.B. that will tell you *exactly* what it's thinking, and it will do so with absolutely no tact whatsoever. The good news, of course, is that the tough love pays off big time, and your timing will improve by leaps and bounds if you use it faithfully.

I'm not saying that you have to use the metronome the entire time you practice. When you're first learning an example and working out the particulars for both hands, it can be kind of annoying to have the thing ticking in the background. But once you have the motions under your fingers and are ready to play the lick in time, the metronome will help make sure that you're not lopsided in your delivery.

Metronome Usage

To make the best use of your practice time, and to improve most rapidly, I recommend following this simple procedure for each exercise that you encounter in this book: Set the metronome at an easy tempo for you. You should be able to practice the exercise flawlessly. If you can't play it flawlessly, slow the metronome down. Once you've decided on a good starting tempo, write it down. This will become your daily log with which you will gauge your progress.

Every day, after warming up at your starting tempo, raise the metronome one notch higher and play the exercise. Record your progress for that day and indicate whether or not you were able to play the exercise successfully and smoothly. Repeat this process every day that you practice. If you reach a tempo that gives you problems, back it off a few notches and start there the next day.

If you're disciplined with this approach, you should notice major improvement in your abilities within a period of a few months. If results come slower for you, just keep in mind that your true goal is to get comfortable with the techniques—not necessarily to play the exercises fast—and that this process cannot be rushed.

The Great Plateau

If you've ever spent time with a disciplined practice regimen such as the one above, you've most likely noticed that sometimes you seem to hit a wall. In my experience, it's very rare that a player is able to steadily move the metronome up a few notches every day, for an extended period of time, with no bumps in the road at all. For whatever reason, he or she will usually reach a plateau at some point and progress will seem to stall. Musicians are hardly unique in this phenomenon; it's also common in sports activities and exercises, such as running, weightlifting, etc.

Eventually, however, if you push through, you'll undoubtedly pierce that ceiling and continue onward. Your brain will figure out what it is that was holding you back, make an adjustment, and things will suddenly click into place. The trick is to provide yourself that opportunity (i.e., soldier on until it happens). Plateaus can be frustrating—I know from experience—but try to remember that it's a temporary situation. It's kind of like trying to remember the name of an actor but you just can't get it, so eventually you give up and forget about it. Lo and behold, three days later, the name pops into your head, seemingly out of nowhere. The same thing applies to guitar technique. You may think you're standing still, but trust me: Your subconscious is still working on the problem behind the scenes.

The solutions may present themselves in surprising ways, too. You may find, for example, that after years of holding the pick a certain way, you (seemingly) accidentally realize that if you just angle your thumb or finger a slightly different way, it becomes much easier. Indeed, it almost seems that we make our most notable progresses in broad jumps, as opposed to slow, steady steps. When viewed on a macro scale, the progress does appear gradual, but when you zoom in, you often find that it's comprised of numerous minor adjustments that you've made to your technique (sometimes subconsciously) along the way that have shoved you forward a few steps at a time.

Define Your Objective

Have you ever heard the expression "Don't serve two masters?" This can apply to guitar technique, as well. Think about your favorite players. Now think about what they're known for. Chances are, very few of them are known for more than one or two unique styles. In other words, if someone can shred Yngwie licks all day long, they most likely aren't going to be bebopping their way through a Charlie Parker tune or weaving a fit of Michael Hedges-like acoustic fingerstyle mastery with the same amount of authority. If someone can chicken-pick a Telecaster like Jerry Reed or Brent Mason, they probably don't go on too many multi-fingered, 64th-note, Steve Vai-like tapping excursions.

This is, of course, not to say that the above scenarios are impossible. There are many players, such as Eric Johnson and Guthrie Govan, who cover many styles remarkably well. But they're definitely in the minority. It's much more common for a player to specialize in one main style and then dabble in others for a bit of variety and uniqueness. So, depending on the amount of time you have available, if your primary goal is to learn to alternate pick like Paul Gilbert or shred the harmonic minor scale like Yngwie, then you'll most likely need to limit your pedal-steel-emulating time. Now, if you have six, seven, or more hours a day to devote to playing, then your aperture of possibilities will certainly widen. But if, like many, you only have an hour or two to devote each day, then you'll probably need to be more selective with your time if you want to make serious progress with your primary goal.

Of course, this is all relative to the guitar. There could be plenty of other variables, too. Do you also sing or play another instrument, like bass or keys? Do you write songs or compose instrumental music? Do you have a home studio and like to record a lot? And what about non-musical hobbies?

There's no one correct method, of course; it's just a matter of deciding what your priorities are. Would you rather be really great at one or two things or pretty good at many things? Both types of players have their place, but it's up to you to decide which you'd like to be. Since you bought this book, I'm going to assume that—for now, at least—your primary goal is to improve your technical prowess on electric guitar in a predominantly rock context, and I will proceed as such. But please feel free to prove me wrong on the side!

Cleanliness Is Key

In order to make sure your playing is clean and solid throughout, I recommend practicing with three different guitar tone setups: 1) with your normal distorted (if you use distortion) tone, 2) with a clean tone, and 3) with your volume rolled all the way off (i.e., unamplified).

- **Distortion:** It's important to practice with distortion because it introduces several variables that aren't present in clean playing. The main one is noise. Aside from feedback and extraneous open strings ringing out (which is much nastier-sounding when using distortion than when using a clean tone), it's also much easier to generate unwanted notes or noise by nudging a neighboring string with either hand. Of course, the flip side is that, since distortion compresses your sound so much (i.e., it evens out your dynamics, or loud and soft playing), it's easier for it to hide some mistakes (such as flubbed or swallowed notes) that would be evident with a cleaner setting.

- **Clean tone:** Playing with a clean tone will make it much easier to detect if you're not hitting every note cleanly. The accents of your picking dynamics are much easier to hear, which means it's also easier to hear if you miss or flub some notes.

- **Unamplified:** This is especially great for hearing flubbed notes and really making sure that you have a clean and clear connection to both the fretboard and the picking motion. However, it's a little harder to hear the individual dynamics from note to note than when playing amplified with a clean tone, which helps to greatly amplify (no pun intended) the differences.

How you'd like to divide your time with regard to tone is up to you. It may make sense to play each and every exercise three different ways, one after the other. Or you may choose to spend an entire day playing with only one tone, changing each day. It doesn't really matter as long as you're spending roughly an equal time on each. I'd say that, if there was one method that could be considered optional at times, it would be the unamplified one. It's still very beneficial, in my opinion, but it's not as critical as the clean and distorted tones are.

Recording Yourself (Taking Your Medicine)

Finally, I recommend that you periodically record yourself playing these exercises (or others) *along with the metronome* (does it need to be said?) to give you a reality check. Again, if you've never done this before, the results may be a bit shocking at first, but that's good; it means that you're hearing the issues and are well on your way to correcting them. I also recommend recording yourself while jamming along to some songs or backing tracks, as this is the goal (playing music) after all! As mentioned above, try recording yourself with various tones (clean, distorted, etc.) to make sure that you're not leaning on anything as a crutch.

Note that, if you have the means, a DAW is particularly helpful because you can see the waveforms and visually see whether or not you're playing evenly within the beat. Sometimes it's easy to overlook some lopsidedness in your playing if the notes on the beat sound in time. But the notes in between the beats matter, too!

A Note on Practicing

There are surprisingly few studies on practice habits and their effectiveness, but the most recent ones suggest that it's better to vary your practice routine. In other words, you don't want to spend an hour Monday working only on alternate picking, an hour Tuesday working only on economy picking, etc. It's better to practice various topics each day. Even further still, studies suggest that the act of frequently *recalling* a skillset is more effective in the long term. Basically, this means that you want to come back to something more than once per session.

For example, if you have an hour to practice on Monday and you want to work on alternate picking, economy picking, and chord vocabulary, instead of spending 20 minutes on each topic, it's better to spend seven minutes on each and repeat that cycle three times. By doing this, you're forcing your brain to recall the alternate-picking movement three times instead of just once. And the science suggests that this leads to more effective progress in the long term. It may not seem that way after one or two days, but if you stick with it, by a few weeks or so, the varied method should overtake the singular method.

Again, this is still a relatively new area of study, so feel free to take it with a grain of salt. But it seems like good advice to me regardless, as it will most likely help to keep practice sessions from becoming boring or stale. It's a good idea to use a timer or stopwatch in this regard—most smartphones have this feature built in—because, as you no doubt know, it's easy to lose track of time when playing the guitar!

ABOUT THE AUDIO

To access the audio examples that accompany this book, simply go to *www.halleonard.com/mylibrary* and enter the code found on page 1. This will grant you instant access to each example.

The accompanying audio provides demonstrations of each example in the book. Most examples are performed at moderate-to-quick tempos for demonstration purposes, as this will give you something to aim for and surpass. These should not be considered starting tempos, however. Start at whatever tempo you need in order to play the exercises cleanly. For the full-band examples, two mixes are provided: one with the lead, and one minus the lead.

All instruments and programming performed by Chad Johnson.

Recorded and mixed at Magnetized World Studio in Anna, Texas.

WARMUP EXERCISES

If you're the type that never reads the manual before using a new piece of equipment, you'll probably be inclined to skip this section. But before you do, please hear me out! Stretching your arms, hands, and fingers before you play can really do wonders if you've never tried it before. Just as an athlete stretches out before exercising, musicians can greatly benefit from the effects of stretching as well. It will improve flexibility and stamina and greatly reduce the risk of injury.

Ideally, the following exercises should be performed daily before each practice session. They don't take that long—less than five minutes—and they can really help prepare your hands, arms, and body. The exercises provide a nice opportunity to clear and focus your mind for the task at hand.

Exercise 1

While extending your left arm out in front with your palm turned up and facing away from you (as if making a "stop" gesture), grab your left-hand fingertips with your right hand and gently pull them towards you. You should feel a gentle burn in your left forearm and fingers. Hold this for 15–20 seconds; then switch hands and repeat the exercise.

Exercise 2

Hold your left arm out again, but this time point your palm towards you. With your right hand, grab the back of your left hand (the side you can't see) and gently pull towards you. You should feel a gentle burn on the opposite side of your forearm than in Exercise 1. Again, hold, switch hands, and repeat.

Exercise 3

While holding your hands together, reach straight up as high as you can. Hold for 15–20 seconds. This will stretch your triceps and back.

Exercise 4

You'll need to stand up for this one. While clutching your hands behind your back, reach back as far as you can, creating a right angle between your back and arms. This will target your biceps and chest. Hold for 15–20 seconds.

That's it. You've covered just about every muscle you'll use in your guitar playing, and you're ready to get started.

CHAPTER 1

ALTERNATE PICKING, PART 1 – EVEN GROUPINGS

The concept of alternate picking is fairly self-explanatory: You simply alternate between downstrokes and upstrokes consistently. It sounds simple enough, but depending on how the notes are arranged on certain strings, there are a few problems that can arise when attempting to use this technique at a brisk tempo. These problems mainly deal with crossing to a new string. There are basically two different scenarios that can occur when crossing strings: Switching after an upstroke and switching after a downstroke. We'll be looking extensively at both in this book, but in this chapter, we'll focus mostly on the former.

Food for Thought

It should be noted that, generally speaking, alternate picking is one of the most widely used picking techniques in a guitarist's arsenal (even those who use economy/sweep picking [see Chapter 3] still have to alternate pick a good deal). Because of this, it's important to develop a relaxed and consistent picking motion. Many times, a certain amount of stamina may be required in order to pick longer passages. In the beginning, it's a good idea to occasionally stop in the middle of these exercises to make sure that you're not tensing any part of your arm, wrist, or hand. Doing so for an extended period of time could result in sore muscles or even injury in extreme cases—not to mention the fact that it could color your phrases with an uptight or uneasy feel.

Four Notes Per String

The first few examples may as well be called "Picking Exercises 101." Probably the most popular exercises that you'll encounter, they're extremely efficient, giving both hands a full workout. This makes them excellent warmup exercises. Granted, they don't sound nice, but the benefit for both hands is worth it. There are two important things to concentrate on here:

1. Playing the notes cleanly (i.e., achieving a nice, clear tone on each note)

2. Playing the notes in time (i.e., not rushing or dragging the beat)

With regard to playing in time, this doesn't just refer to making sure that the first note in each beat lines up with the metronome (because you *will* be using your metronome!); it also refers to the notes in each beat. Make sure that you're not rushing through the first three, for instance, and lagging on the last one. There should be no lopsidedness at all. If it helps at first, you can set your metronome to tick twice as fast, as eighth notes (or even 16th notes), to make sure that you're playing evenly through the beat. And just in case it's not obvious, be sure to use all four fret-hand fingers here, one finger per fret.

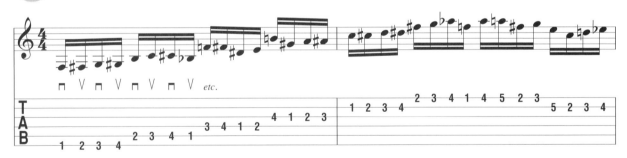

Track 2 is very similar to Track 1, but the order of the notes changes on each string. We begin with the first finger on string 6, then the second finger on string 5, then the third finger on string 4, etc. The quickest way to get this is probably just to memorize the following left-hand pattern: 1–2–3–4, 2–3–4–1, 3–4–1–2, 4–1–2–3.

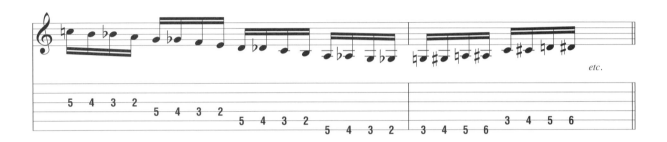

Track 3 simply reverses the process of Track 2. Here, we're descending through the four-note pattern on each string: 4–3–2–1, 3–2–1–4, 2–1–4–3, 1–4–3–2.

TRACK 3

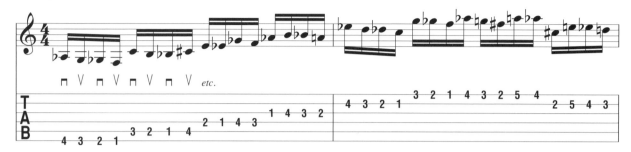

Look Both Ways Before Crossing the... Strings

When playing four notes per string, as with the previous exercises, we encounter two types of string-crossing: Inside picking and outside picking. When ascending through the strings (i.e., moving from string 6 to string 1), *inside picking* is used. The name stems from the fact that your pick stays "inside" the two strings while crossing. In this case, we have an upstroke on the sixth string moving to a downstroke on the fifth string. So the pick is "inside" the 6–5 string group. Many players generally consider this technique to be the more difficult of the two.

When descending from string 1 to string 6, we encounter *outside picking*. After picking the last note on string 1 with an upstroke, our pick moves over string 2 in order to attack it with a downstroke. So the pick is "outside" the 1–2 string group. This usually feels more natural to most players.

So, why is that? Well, it's a question of momentum. During inside picking, you're moving away from the next string that you're going to pick. Think about it: If you pick string 6 with an upstroke, your pick will be *above* string 6; then you need to come back down—making sure that you don't nudge string 6 on the way—to pick string 5 with a downstroke. With outside picking, you're already moving in the right direction. If you pick string 1 with an upstroke, your pick is already travelling toward string 2.

There's actually a bit more to it than that, depending upon the type of lick being played. We'll look more at this idea as we progress through the book. This may sound like excessive analysis for something that seems so small, but make no mistake: This is a very real issue that plagues many players. In fact, it's no stretch at all to say that some very well-known players—including Yngwie Malmsteen and Eric Johnson, to name a few—have tailored much of their picking/playing technique to deal with this problem. We'll talk more about that idea in a bit.

For now, play through the previous examples again and note how different each method (inside vs. outside) feels.

Next, we'll double up on the notes we played during Track 1. This may feel awkward at first because your hands are no longer working in a one-on-one relationship, so be sure that you're cleanly articulating every note. It's very easy to get out of sync when playing each note more than once. Technically, this isn't four notes per string anymore (it's eight), but I'm fudging the rules a bit because this is a very specific skill that needs to be practiced.

TRACK 4

"Pick" a Method That Works for You

There are a lot of different ways to hold the pick, and you can find ample evidence of this in the playing of some of the best pickers around. However, there are two aspects of pick-holding that I feel deserve special attention with regard to playing fast: pick angling and pick slanting.

Pick Angling

It's fairly safe to say that the vast majority of chops-oriented guitar players tend to angle the pick somewhat when playing. This can be more subtle, as with Steve Morse, or it can be a bit more pronounced, as with

Paul Gilbert or Yngwie Malmsteen. Most players angle the pick so that the front edge (i.e., the one closer to the neck of the guitar) is closer to the ground. However, there are some players, such as Journey rocker Neal Schon, virtuoso jazzman George Benson, and the late technical superfreak Shawn Lane, who angle/angled it in the other direction, with the front edge farther from the ground.

Typical pick angle

Alternate (reverse) pick angle

The goal for both methods is the same: To reduce the friction of the pick when moving through a string. It's very easy to conduct an experiment to test this. Just try holding the pick at various angles as you play. Starting from directly parallel to the string, begin rotating the pick off-axis. You'll most likely notice that the pick glides through the string easier when it's angled a bit. Try varying the angle until you find the position that's most comfortable for you. This will be slightly different for everyone, depending on the size and proportion of your hand and fingers.

The same can be said for the overall picking-hand technique. If you look at 10 different players, you'll likely see 10 different-looking pick hands. Some players, like Paul Gilbert, gently curl the other fingers inward (as if holding a ball), while others, like George Lynch and Michael Angelo Batio, fan them out to varying degrees. Marty Friedman curls the fingers up tightly and pronates his wrist, while Steve Vai collapses his thumb joint but still angles his pick normally (as opposed to George Benson, who also collapses the thumb but uses the reverse angle). This is all to say that there's obviously not one "proper" method for holding the pick, as all of the above-mentioned players are top-rated pickers who use completely different methods.

Pick Slanting

The second aspect of pick technique is what's sometimes called *pick slanting*. This refers to the pushing forward (or pulling back) of the top edge of the pick so that it's no longer perpendicular to the body of the guitar. It's a bit difficult to explain, so in this case, a picture is worth a thousand words.

Forward pick slanting

Backward pick slanting

If you spend some time closely watching the pick hand of speedy players, you'll most likely notice them slightly changing their pick posture to facilitate the type of lick they're playing. This can be very subtle in some players—such as the thumb slightly bending back and forth in the case of Paul Gilbert—or, in the case of Frank Gambale, it can be quite obvious. It's a sign that the player is altering the angle or slant of the pick to aid in the task at hand. It's sometimes very difficult to see at normal speed, but if you can slow down video, it's always there in some fashion.

So, what does this all mean for your average licks? Well, it means that you can make things easier for yourself by slanting the pick to suit the particular lick. The slant doesn't have to be as extreme as shown in the photos; some players tend to slant the pick in one particular direction almost exclusively, and this definitely has an effect of the types of lines that they play frequently and the ones they tend to avoid.

Slanting the pick forward (some people also call this "downward" pick slanting) facilitates changing to a new string after an upstroke because the pick is above the plane of the strings after an upstroke.

Yngwie Malmsteen is a prime example of someone who slants the pick forward almost exclusively, and he's practically built his entire technique around it, employing pull-offs when necessary so that he's always changing strings after an upstroke—when playing lightning fast, that is. Marty Friedman also plays with an extreme forward slant. We'll look more at this idea soon.

After an upstroke on the G string with forward pick slanting

Conversely, slanting the pick backward (some people also call this "upward" pick slanting) facilitates changing strings after a downstroke, because the pick is above the plane of the strings after a downstroke.

There aren't many players who use backward slanting exclusively—most likely because it feels a bit less natural—but many players who use consistent alternate picking for certain phrases, such as Paul Gilbert, employ it when necessary to facilitate the picking.

To demonstrate this, let's take a look at two examples. The first is a simple C major scale fragment on strings 1 and 2. It's arranged with four notes on each string, and we're starting with a downstroke. Notice that we're always changing strings after an upstroke, which means that forward pick slanting will be easier.

After a downstroke on the G string with backward pick slanting

 TRACK 5

Now let's shift everything by one note. We're going to be playing the exact same series of eight notes, but this time, we'll put the second note of Track 5, the A note, on the downbeat. This will make it much more difficult when using forward pick slanting because, after picking the third note, A, with a downstroke, your pick would be buried below the first string and then have to hop over it to pick the second string with an upstroke. The solution is to slant the pick backward for this type of lick.

 **TRACK 6**

It should be mentioned that you could achieve the same effect by starting Track 5 with an upstroke. In fact, that's great pick-slanting practice for any lick, as it will effectively reverse the slanting motions necessary to play the lick. However, in the spirit of trying to make practicing more musical, I prefer to shift the pattern by one note, as this not only feels the same to your hands, but it also provides a different musical effect, which can help with the inherent monotony in practicing these types of things.

To feel the difference, try playing Tracks 5 and 6 with both types of slanting. In one way, the pick will fight you, but with the other way, it will work with you. Looking back at Tracks 1–4, all of them cross strings after an upstroke, which means they're best served with forward pick slanting. Go back now and try them again, keeping this in mind. Again, the amount of slant doesn't need to be severe; in fact, it's barely perceptible in some players, such as Michael Angelo Batio. In Eric Johnson's playing, however, the forward pick slant (he, like Yngwie, rarely uses backward slanting) is much more noticeable.

Let's look at two more examples that employ a bit of position-shifting in the fret hand to raise the bar a bit. This first one is in G and uses a two-beat G major scale fragment that repeats in three octaves. We're starting on string 6 and working our way up, picking four notes on each string, just as in Tracks 1–3. So it's nothing new for the picking hand. But the position shifts in the fret hand add the element of synchronization between the hands. Practice the shifts slowly at first and work the tempo up gradually. Make sure that you're not getting a lopsided sound (i.e., playing each fragment at tempo but hesitating after each shift).

 **TRACK 7**

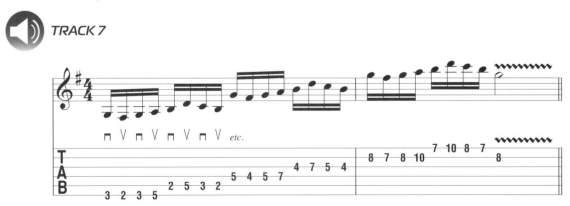

We reverse directions in the following C minor lick and progress from string 1 to string 6, picking four notes on each. Sometimes shifting down can feel different than shifting up to some people. I generally prefer to shift down, for some reason. Nevertheless, both moves need to be practiced!

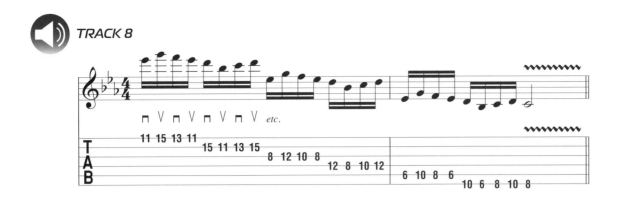

Two Notes Per String

Now let's check out playing two notes per string with alternate picking. What about three notes per string, you ask? Good question. We're going to look at that in the next chapter because there are other picking options available when using an odd number of notes (one, three, five, etc.) on each string. When playing an even number of notes (two, four, etc.) per string, alternate picking is the only option—when playing fast, that is.

Compared to four notes per string, two notes per string doesn't involve different mechanics, but your picking hand will be moving through the strings much more fluently when moving in one direction continuously, which demands attention. It will likely feel less grounded at first than playing four notes per string. As with every technique, it will become more comfortable with steady practice.

When you talk two notes per string, the pentatonic scale immediately comes to mind. Mastered beyond belief by Eric Johnson and Zakk Wylde, to name a few, these scales are generally easy for the fretting hand but can be quite problematic for the picking hand, depending on the direction you're moving and on which stroke (up or down) you begin. Track 9 presents the best possible scenario: an uninterrupted stream of two notes per string. We're just working from a D minor pentatonic box shape on the low three strings. Starting with a downstroke, it's forward pick slanting all the way.

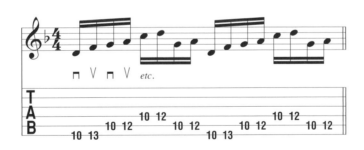

To make this a great exercise for the fret hand, as well, we can alter the pattern of notes on strings 5 and 4. This means that you'll need to roll your fret-hand index and ring fingers on frets 10 and 12, respectively. Make sure that the notes aren't bleeding together when you do this.

OK, now let's throw a monkey wrench into things again, similar to Track 6. As long as you keep an even number of notes on a string—like two or four, etc.—you can keep your pick slanted the same way (forward, in this case) to gain an advantage when crossing strings. But all it takes is one odd set of notes to change that. In this example, we're running up the D minor pentatonic scale with two notes per string as usual, but when we get to string 2, we play only one note on it and then turn back around to descend to where we started. This means that, on the way down, we're changing strings after a *downstroke*, which will feel very different. What does this mean? It means that you'll need to alternate between forward pick slanting while ascending on beats 1–2 and backward pick slanting while descending on beats 3–4.

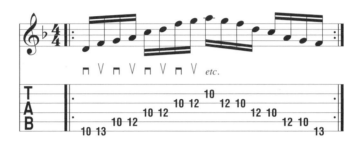

Of course, you can play many other things besides pentatonic scales with two notes per string. Seventh-chord arpeggios are another common application. Here's an exercise that will really work the often-neglected middle and pinky fingers on the fret hand. We're alternating between Amaj7 and E7 arpeggios played on two-note string groups. The same shapes are transposed up and played in three different octaves.

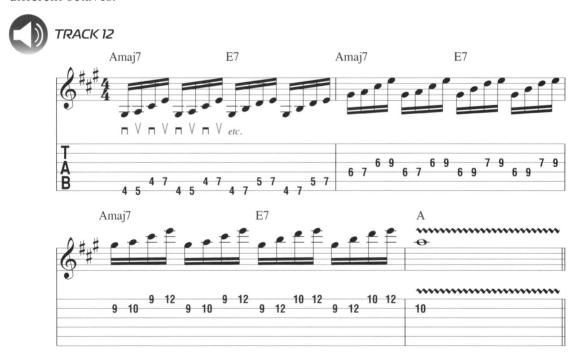

And next is a nice-sounding arpeggio sequence in the opposite direction. We're alternating between Cm7 and G7 arpeggios, but we've switched up the order of the notes here so that we begin with only one note on string 2. The shapes are still two notes per string, but by changing the order of notes like this, we'll be changing strings mostly after downstrokes, which means we need to slant the pick backwards. The one exception to this is the last note of each measure (i.e., the last note of beat 4). This is an upstroke note, and afterward we're skipping a string to reach down for the next octave. Therefore, you'll want to slightly roll the pick to a forward slant for this move, resuming with a backward slant after you begin the sequence again in the lower octave. This exercise is also great for the fret hand because we're working all four fingers. It gets a little stretchy in measure 3, so be sure to keep your thumb behind the neck.

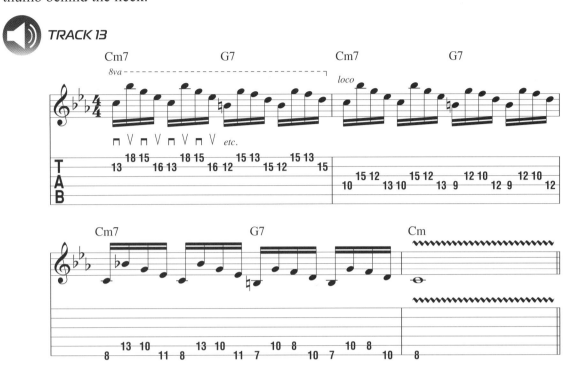

Summary

Again, this may seem like a superfluous amount of fuss over alternate picking. I mean… you just alternate down and up for Pete's sake, right?! Well, yes and no. I'm sure you've noticed over the years that certain licks or patterns come easier for your picking hand while others are more troublesome. I'd be willing to bet that most of the problem licks largely have to do with string crossing. You have two options in this regard. You can:

- **Avoid the phrases that trouble you and/or find other methods to play them:** Many players use this approach, and it's in no way a cop out; it's just an alternate solution to a problem. If you get creative, you can find ways to play basically the same thing but without encountering the technical stopping blocks that normally prevent you from playing a certain lick. This can include the use of economy picking (which we'll look at later), strategically placed legato articulations, alternate fret-hand fingerings, or a combination of all the above. We'll be looking at each of these ideas at some point in this book.

- **Study and identify exactly what the problem is and learn how to adjust for it:** This is what pick slanting is about. If you closely watch your pick hand when you play—or, better yet, if you can film yourself playing quickly and then slow it down—you'll notice the slight moves you need to make when crossing strings. By slanting our pick one way or the other, we can make the job of string crossing much easier.

Applied Techniques

Now let's put these tools to use with some licks that employ what we've worked on. All of these licks will feature even note groupings and will therefore include string crossing after an upstroke. This means that forward pick slanting can be used throughout.

Our first lick comes from D minor pentatonic and begins in fifth position. After running straight up the scale through one octave, we begin climbing the neck with strings 4 and 3 in two-note groupings until we reach 12th/13th position. The hardest part here is making all of the position shifts clean, so pay extra attention to them.

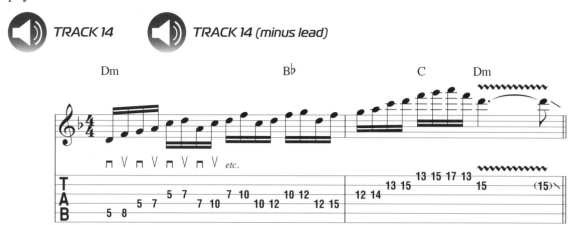

Here, we're working entirely out of seventh position. Using a symmetrical fingering involving frets 7, 9, and 10 on strings 1–4, we move a repeated sextuplet phrase down a string group three times, resulting in a hybrid phrase from B Dorian and the B blues scale. We finish it off with a sextuplet run down the B minor pentatonic scale, which is a favorite of players like Eric Johnson and Joe Bonamassa.

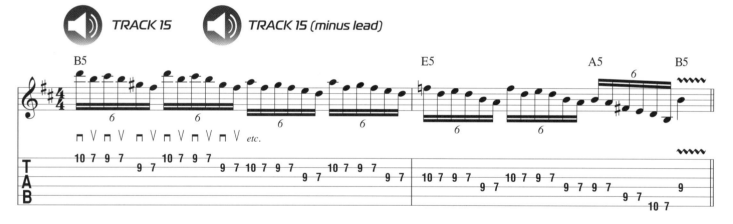

This is another pentatonic tour de force that moves through several different positions during the descent, this time in C♯ minor. Be sure that you're not rushing or dragging the position shifts and that every note is ringing out clearly.

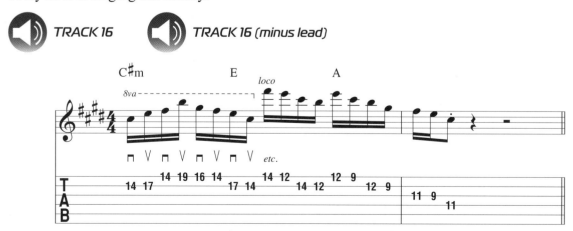

This example in A minor has kind of a Paul Gilbert sound and combines two different ascending sequence ideas. First up is a 1–2–3–1 idea (A–B–C–A), followed by a 2–3–4–5 one (B–C–D–E). After each two-beat group, we shift up and begin the idea again at the new pitch level. It takes place entirely on strings 4 and 3. The picking for this one should feel fairly simple, but the shifts can be troublesome, so make sure that you're executing them cleanly.

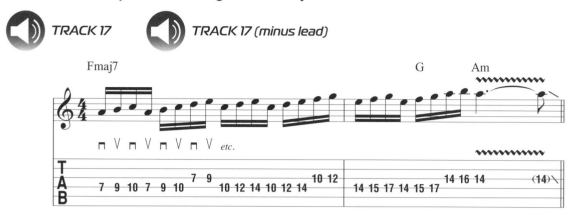

Here's an interesting sextuplet lick in D that climbs up strings 3 and 2. It's kind of the opposite idea, picking-wise, to that of Track 15. You'll get some good practice rolling your fret-hand index finger on this one, as well.

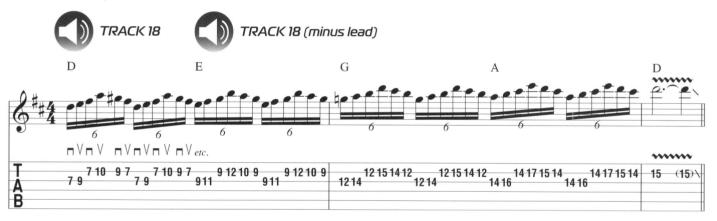

Finally, in this last lick, we'll get some practice with multiple picks for each note. While playing an eighth-note melody in G minor with our fret hand, we're picking steady sextuplets, which equates to three picks for every note. Notice that we've arranged the fret-hand notes so that we still have an even number of notes on each string (six on string 6, 12 on string 5, and six on string 4). Be sure that you're picking each note only three times. This shouldn't turn into a haphazard tremolo lick in the picking hand. Strive for complete accuracy in this regard.

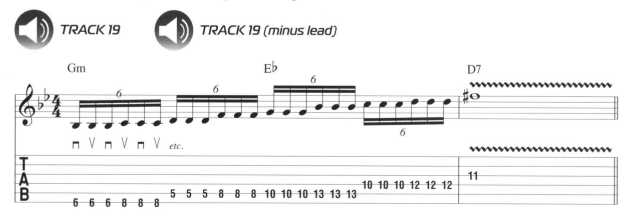

CHAPTER 2

ALTERNATE PICKING, PART 2 – ODD AND MIXED GROUPINGS

In Chapter 1, we mostly looked at licks that used an even number of notes on each string. This meant that we crossed strings after an upstroke so we could make the string crossing easier by slanting the pick forward, thereby bringing our pick above the plane of the strings after an upstroke. In this chapter, that won't be the case anymore.

Odd Groupings

When we have an odd number of notes on each string, we'll no longer be crossing strings after upstrokes exclusively. Indeed, if we play an odd group of notes on every string (it doesn't matter if it's one, three, five, etc.), we'll be alternating between down- and upstrokes every time we cross strings. The most obvious example of this is three-notes-per-string scale patterns. Take this C major scale form, for instance:

C Major Scale

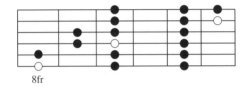

8fr

If you use strict alternate picking, it will look like this:

- **String 6:** down–up–down
- **String 5:** up–down–up
- **String 4:** down–up–down
- **String 3:** up–down–up
- **String 2:** down–up–down
- **String 1:** up–down–up

If you play through this shape at a moderate tempo and watch your pick hand very closely, you'll most likely see your hand jump ever so slightly when moving from string 6 to string 5, from string 4 to string 3, and from string 2 to string 1. This is because you're going from a downstroke on one string to an upstroke on the next. The majority of players, if they slant the pick at all, tend to slant it forward a bit because it feels more natural (to slant it backward is to fight gravity a bit). This means that, after playing string 6 with a downstroke, your pick is going to be slightly below the plane of the strings when it heads toward string 5. In order to pick string 5 with an upstroke, then, you have to hop over it first, and this is why we see the slight jump in our pick hand.

This is simply not easy to do quickly, and it's the primary reason why so few players have mastered three-notes-per-string scales the way Paul Gilbert and Michael Angelo Batio have. Although Yngwie does make use of three-notes-per-string patterns a good deal of the time, he does not do so in the way that Gilbert and Batio do (i.e., he doesn't dwell on them, moving them up and down the neck to different positions, and he doesn't play them with strict alternate picking).

"Tip" of the Day

So, what's the solution to doing this at super-fast speeds? We need to minimize this jumping motion and smooth it out so that it's more of a slight wobble. This is accomplished by alternating our pick slanting throughout the line. I'm talking about a really minor adjustment here. Therefore, when playing three-notes-per-string scales with alternate picking, I really aim to keep the pick fairly perpendicular (i.e., no pick slanting) and concentrate on using only the *very tip* of the pick. The closer your picking is to the tip, the less slanting/hopping you'll need to do in order to clear the strings when crossing them. Again, if you ever see close-up pick-hand video of someone like Batio, you'll see that he's using the very tip of the pick.

So let's give it a spin with this A major scale fragment. We're starting from the seventh degree instead of the root because it makes for a more musical phrase, suggesting a three-beat dominant V chord (E7) that resolves to the I chord (A) on beat 4.

TRACK 20

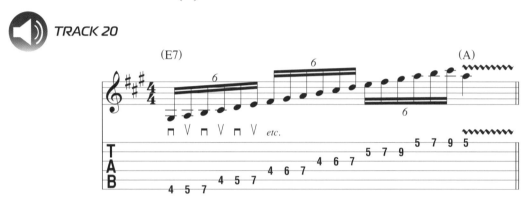

Now let's try the descending version of this scale. We'll move up to the next position and start with the D note at fret 10. For the final, low G♯ note, you'll need to shift your first finger down one fret.

TRACK 21

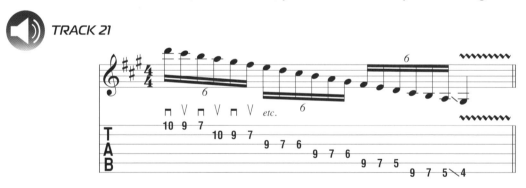

Seventh-chord arpeggios work nicely for three-notes-per-string patterns as well. Here's a nice one that climbs up a B♭7 pattern and descends through E♭maj7. Remember to use the tip of the pick!

TRACK 22

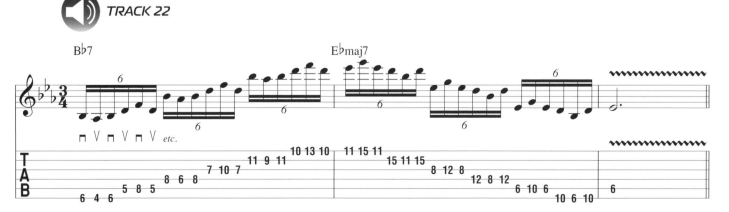

And here's one that sounds a bit outside. We're ascending through a D major arpeggio, but we're using a concept called *enclosure*—playing notes a half step above and a half step below the target note. This is an excellent shifting exercise for the fret hand.

 **TRACK 23**

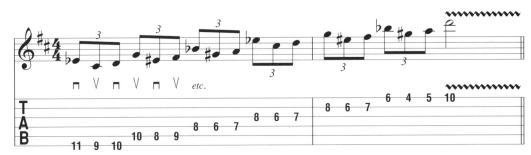

Finally, here's a three-notes-per-string scale pattern in C Dorian that ascends from string 6 to string 1 but with *descending* three-note fragments on each string. Pay close attention to the rhythm when playing this one and make sure it's not lopsided-sounding.

 **TRACK 24**

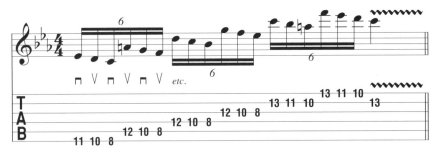

Taking Advantage When You Can

Although it doesn't involve any string crossing, sequence licks along one string like this next one make great practice for synchronizing the hands while shifting. Since you don't have to worry about moving to another string, you can concentrate solely on the timing of the pick and fret hand working together through several position shifts without any other interruptions.

 **TRACK 25**

Concentrate on keeping your pick- and fret-hand movements small and concise; you don't want a bunch of wasted motion. Also, remember to experiment with different pick angles on licks like these to see what works best for you. When you don't have to worry about string crossing, you can tailor your technique to take advantage of that.

A lot of times, we have this utopic vision of technique, thinking that we should be able to play anything and everything at the same speed, etc. But, if the great players of the past and present have taught us anything, it's that this is not the case. Most players have many "pet licks" for which they're known, and it's no surprise. It's because they've found their strengths and exploit them. You can practice slamming your fist against a wall all you want in the hopes that it eventually won't hurt anymore, or you can just put on some boxing gloves. If the gloves are there, use them!

Here's another nice grouping to practice: three notes on one string and one on another. We're working entirely on strings 2 and 1 here in the key of E minor. Every two beats, we move up a scale degree, but we're alternating between playing an ascending run in one position and a descending run in the next. At the end, we collapse the two-beat idea into one-beat chunks, immediately following the descending lick on beat 3 of measure 2 with an ascending one on beat 4 to resolve the lick nicely. You'll get some nice practice rolling your index finger here, as well as your pinky (beats 3 and 4 of measure 1).

TRACK 26

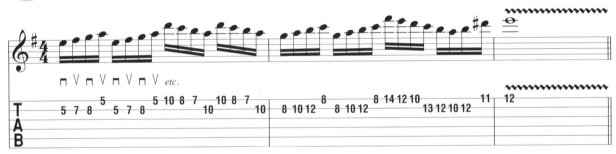

Mixed Groupings

What I call "mixed groupings" is basically just alternate picking freestyle, meaning it can be any number of notes on a string at any time. These aren't formulaic licks derived from arranging groups of notes carefully on a string; they're a mixed bag of "anything goes" and can therefore present some real technical challenges for the alternate-picker. However, that's not to say that you can't do anything to make them easier.

A classic example of this is a descending scale sequence in groups of four. If you remain in one basic position in the fret hand and descend through a three-notes-per-string shape, you'll be repeating a picking pattern comprised of three segments:

- Three notes on the higher-pitched string and one on the lower-pitched (labeled A)

- Two notes on the higher-pitched string and two on the lower-pitched (labeled B)

- One note on the higher-pitched string and three on the lower-pitched (labeled C)

Arranged on two strings, this pattern will work its way down in pairs of strings over and over. Check it out in this seventh-position G major scale sequence, starting with the 5th, D.

 *TRACK 27*

Be sure to note the recurring pattern of notes arranged on each string pair: 3/1–2/2–1/3, 3/1–2/2–1/3, over and over. It's important to be aware of this so you can isolate the issues you may be having. If you know the picking pattern repeats like this, then you know that you really only need to solve the problem once. After that, the same fix will apply to each repetition.

Time for Some Detective Work

As with the wall-punching analogy earlier, sometimes endless repetition or brute force is not enough. Sometimes a little sleuthing is more effective. For example, I generally play with more of a forward pick slant, so lines that are arranged in even notes per string are usually easy for me, whereas lines like the previous one—with lots of odd groupings—are often troublesome for me. After some experimentation and close examination, I discovered that my biggest problem occurred at the first note of the C chunk. I tended to also play that note with a forward pick slant and, as a result, I would often hit the string again while trying to move past it on the way to the next upstroke. Chunk B never bothers me because it lines up perfectly with forward pick slanting (i.e., crossing strings after an upstroke). And I think chunk A doesn't bother me as much as chunk C because the problematic string cross—a downstroke on a higher-pitched string followed by an upstroke on the lower-pitched one—occurs at the end of the beat and is therefore accented less. I think I tend to want to pick the first note of the C chunk harder (as an accent) because it's on the beat, but that makes for a less-efficient stroke, which makes it harder to recover from.

All this is to say that I realized I needed to consciously slant the pick backward a bit at those times to help in clearing the string. I also realized that it helps me to increase the angle of the pick a bit in these kinds of lines. Once I became aware of those two main things, the sequence became playable for me. I could have practiced the lick the old way until I was blue in the face, but I never would have been able to clear that string quickly enough without making the adjustment I did. Keep this in mind the next time you're struggling with a phrase. Identifying the problem is the first step to finding the solution.

This E Dorian lick is another good example of this type of troublesome inside string-crossing. However, when I try to switch the picking and start with an upstroke, although my pick may not feel as "trapped," I still can't really play it any faster. (Actually, I can play it faster as written, probably because I'm not as accustomed to starting a lick with an upstroke.) Again, it wasn't until I spent some time examining the trouble spots and making adjustments that I was able to speed it up a good bit. In my case, it was beat 3 that was tripping me up, so I had to make a conscious effort once again to slant the pick backward at that spot (and again on beat 4).

TRACK 28

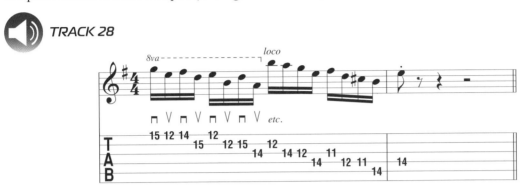

This is not to say that you'll have to do this for every single new lick you learn. But you may have to do it with every new technical challenge you encounter. Think of licks or phrases as sentences and new techniques as new words: When you hear a new word, you may have to look it up in the dictionary to see what it means. But most new sentences you hear don't contain new words, just like most licks you encounter won't contain new technical challenges. This detective work (i.e., isolating trouble spots in sequences or licks) will pay dividends down the line when you come across another lick that contains the same type of technical challenge.

Here's a very scalar lick in A major that features one position shift at the end. The general tendency is to want to rush the shift with the fret hand, so make sure that you're not getting out of sync.

TRACK 29

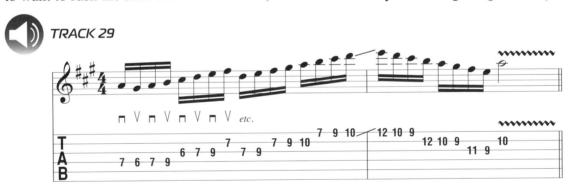

Summary

Alternate-picking odd or mixed groupings of notes on each string presents more technical challenges than even groupings simply because you can't orientate your pick slant in one advantageous way and leave it there; you either have to slightly alter your slant back and forth throughout the lick or—if you want to leave it slanted forward the whole time—hop over a string when crossing to a new one after an upstroke. I personally prefer the former method, but you may not. Again, we're talking about very small moves here that are hard to notice when playing fast, but there's no way around it. If you're using a downstroke on string 6 and you're following it with an upstroke on string 5, you either have to hop string 5 or have your pick slanted so that it clears it automatically. There's just no other option when using alternate picking. Some players learn how to do this subconsciously and don't even realize how they're doing what they're doing, but others need a little help getting there. And that's where this book comes in!

Applied Techniques

Let's check out some licks that make use of these odd groupings. This first one is in C minor and takes place entirely in eighth position, mixing even and odd groupings throughout. If you're a forward pick-slanter, this lick will fight you all the way as notated (i.e., beginning on a downstroke). That's because it was specifically designed so that almost every single string cross occurs after a downstroke, save for the last notes of beats 2 and 4. This means that, if you play it with a forward pick slant, you're going to have to hop over all those string crosses. The solution to this is to use backward pick slanting for this lick. I consciously slant my pick backward a bit for the entire lick, reverting to my natural forward slant only for the very last note. Alternatively, you could begin the lick on an upstroke and use forward pick slanting throughout. You would only have two string hops in the entire lick, which occur at the aforementioned spots.

TRACK 30   TRACK 30 (minus lead)

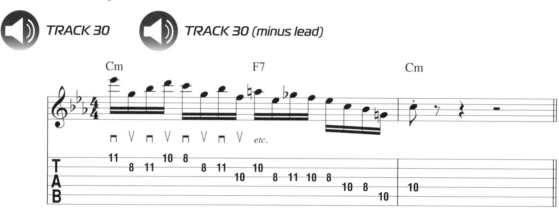

This one is built from G Dorian and also features mixed groupings. At the end of beat 2, we're moving from string 2 through only one note on string 3 on the way to string 4. This is something we haven't done yet, but the same logic applies. You'll need to alternate your pick slant as you progress through the move.

TRACK 31   TRACK 31 (minus lead)

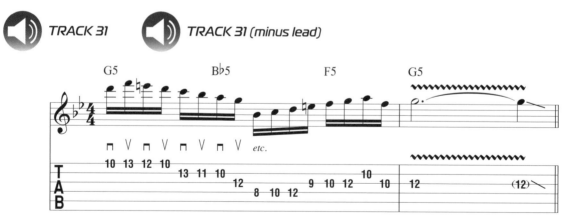

Next up is a neoclassical-sounding lick from the F♯ harmonic minor scale, with the ♭5th (or ♯4th) thrown in at the end for color. You'll get lots of index and middle finger practice on the fret hand here. Picking-wise, this is no different than an ascending three-notes-per-string scale, but the position shifts add an extra layer of difficulty.

This next lick is a fun one in G major that features a lot of chromatic notes. It's mostly based in seventh position and features mixed note groupings throughout.

TRACK 33   TRACK 33 (minus lead)

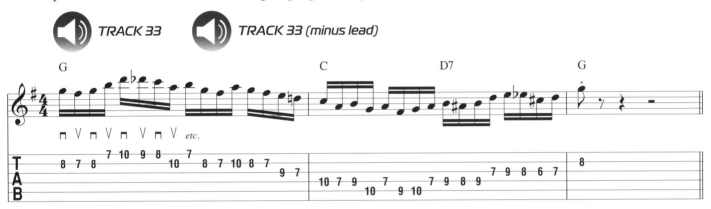

Our last lick for this chapter is very formulaic, with the same number of notes on each string, similar to Track 32. However, instead of three notes per string, we're picking five notes per string as quintuplets (i.e., five notes per beat). This will feel strange to you if you've never done it before, and it'll take a while to learn how to feel the rhythm. Picking-wise, it's not really any different than picking three notes per string, save for the fact that we're adding an extra downstroke and upstroke on each string.

TRACK 34   TRACK 34 (minus lead)

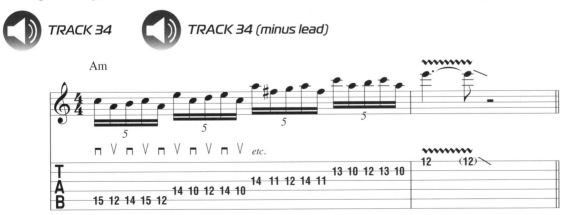

CHAPTER 3

ECONOMY AND SWEEP PICKING

We've now reached the first crossroads of the book. In Chapters 1 and 2, we looked at all the ins and outs of alternate picking (i.e., its technical challenges and ways to help overcome them), but we always had one thing in common: you alternate downstrokes and upstrokes without fail. Is this the only way to pick fast? Absolutely not! Enter economy picking.

The term *economy picking* refers to picking through two adjacent strings with one continuous downstroke (when ascending) or upstroke (when descending). The "economy picking" term is commonly applied to scalar playing, whereby you're only using the technique when crossing to the next, adjacent string. But when you apply this technique to crossing two strings or more, most people call it *sweep picking*. Some people, however, don't make a distinction between the two. Technically speaking, they work on the same exact principle: using one continuous stroke when crossing strings. Therefore, I may refer to either term interchangeably.

To hear complete mastery of this technique, check out Frank Gambale (he's played with Chick Corea's Elektric Band, among many others) and Marshall Harrison (search for him on YouTube), as both guitarists are absolute monsters.

The Basic Idea: Three Notes Per String

One of the most common applications of economy picking is playing three-notes-per-string scales (we'll look at the other most-common application, arpeggios, soon). Let's check this out with our eighth-position C major scale form that begins on string 6.

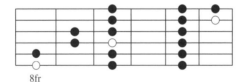

To play this with economy picking, we use a pattern of down–up–down, down–up–down, down–up–down, etc. In detail, it looks like this:

- Pick the first C note (string 6, fret 8) with a downstroke and the following D note (fret 10) with an upstroke.

- Next, pick the E note (fret 12) with a downstroke and then let the pick continue downward to rest (very briefly) against string 5.

- Pick the F note on string 5 (fret 8) with a downstroke and the following G note (fret 10) with an upstroke.

- Pick the following A note (fret 12) with a downstroke and then let the pick continue downward to rest against string 4, etc.

- Continue working through the rest of the strings the same way. When descending, it's the exact opposite: up–down–up, up–down–up, etc.

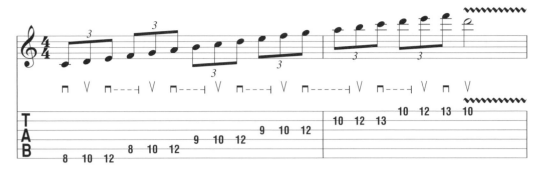

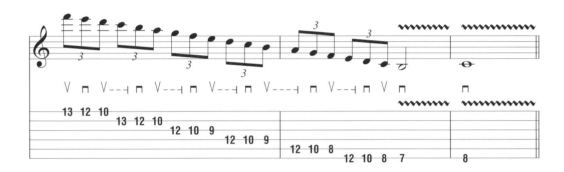

If you've never tried this before, it will feel terribly weird at first. This is perfectly normal for someone who's used alternate picking exclusively (I can tell you that from experience!). The most difficult aspect for most newcomers to this method is usually getting both hands in sync when moving to the new string. This is simply a matter of coordination and will take some time to sort out. I can tell you, though, that in my experience, most players tend to be early with the pick on the new string—in other words, the second string of the mini-sweep.

This can usually be confirmed by simply muting the strings with the fretting hand and concentrating solely on the picking. For instance, try the following exercise:

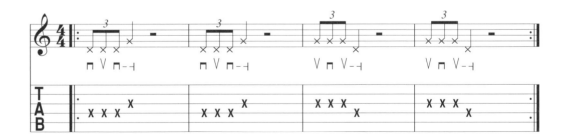

When you're just starting out with economy picking, instead of an even "duh-duh-duh-duh," it's not uncommon for that rhythm to sound closer to "duh-duh-*flppbb*," whereby the last two notes are smeared together like a grace note. So take your time and work on this exercise first, making sure that it's played in time before adding notes with the fret hand.

Pondering Pick Position

If you watch players who use economy picking extensively, such as Frank Gambale, you'll notice that most of them clearly adjust the angle or orientation of their pick, depending on whether they're ascending or descending through the strings. And this makes sense when you think about it: If you're only going to be picking in one direction for a period of time, why not make it easier for yourself? So, feel free to experiment in this regard, especially when playing through three-notes-per-string scales like the previous example in C major. It shouldn't be easy going one way and difficult the other way; it should be easy going both ways.

Interestingly, this is very likely why players like Eric Johnson and Yngwie Malmsteen seem to only use economy picking (when playing fast) on downstrokes. They both use a forward pick-slanting grip by default, which works great for economy picking when ascending but will fight you terribly when descending. Thus, since they decided not to alter their pick grip, they most likely engineered their technique around this fact. The late, great jazz virtuoso Joe Pass used economy picking only when ascending, too, but he even took the idea further: He generally used a downstroke for the first note of *any* string, whether he was ascending or descending. So, when playing three notes per string, for example, he would pick down–up–down, down–up–down, etc. when ascending. But he would also pick down–up–down, down–up-down, etc. when descending, hopping over the string to start each lower-pitched string on a downstroke! At very fast tempos, he would most likely add a legato note to ease the burden on his picking hand if necessary. Considering this, and the fact that he would rarely just play up or down a three-notes-per-string scale for long (his lines were usually a bit more varied than that!), he was able to do all he needed to do.

Now that you've seen how you can apply economy picking to the C major scale when arranged in a three-notes-per-string pattern, you should try it out with lots of different scales/modes to get a feel for it. Try it with Dorian, Mixolydian, harmonic minor, etc. You can find three-notes-per-string fingerings for all of these scales all over the internet if you don't know them already, so give it a shot!

Let's take a look at some classic examples of three-notes-per-string economy picking.

 TRACK 36

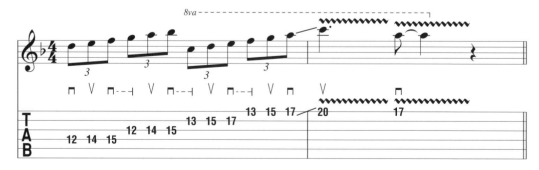

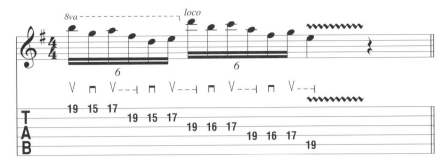

Two Notes Per String

Many people hear "two notes per string" and automatically think that economy picking can't be employed because you have an even number of notes. But you certainly can employ it if you continuously move back and forth between two strings, as these next examples demonstrate. With this type of lick, it's much harder to angle the pick specifically for each direction because you're alternating directions constantly. So, I generally use a neutral pick slant (neither forward nor backward) for these types of licks.

Here's an example of this idea with an E minor pentatonic line. Be sure that the tempo is steady and nothing sounds lopsided before you build up the speed. Starting on a downstroke, the picking pattern will be **down**–up–up–down–**down**–up–up–down, etc.

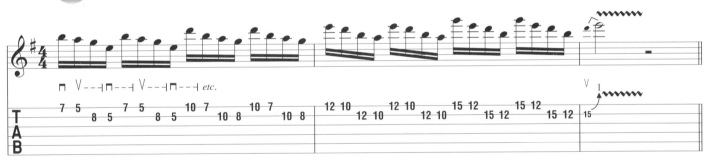

And here's a cool pattern in D Mixolydian that uses the same picking pattern as the previous example. There are some tricky position shifts in this one, so take your time working it up to speed.

Three-One-Three-One and the Mini-Sweep

Another very useful note arrangement for economy picking is three notes on one string alternated with one note on another string. This way, you can play down–up–down, continue to the next string with a downstroke, and then continue again with another downstroke to start the next down–up–down picking pattern. One popular application of this is the minor pentatonic scale. Since you can't use economy picking to play through a normal two-notes-per-string pentatonic shape, you can rearrange the notes and add a bit of fret-hand stretching to accomplish the same thing. Here's an example with the D minor pentatonic scale.

 TRACK 40

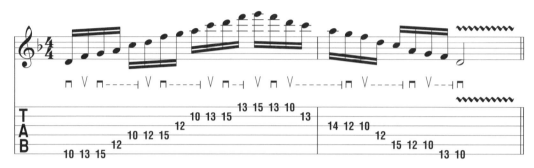

Some people call this a "mini-sweep" because you're sweeping across three strings at once. Here's another application of the same idea with a G major pentatonic line that repeats in three octaves.

 TRACK 41

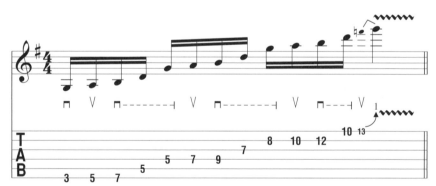

And these lines don't always have to be so formulaic, either. By mixing up the order of the notes, you can get some nice angular-sounding phrases. Here's an example of that with a descending line in E minor.

 TRACK 42

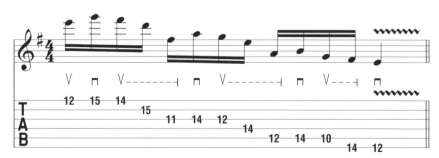

Of course, one of the most common applications of the "mini-sweep" is the arpeggio. You can hear Yngwie often making use of this idea on the top three strings. After sweeping through strings 3–1, notice the use of a pull-off on string 1. This is critical with respect to allowing the picking pattern to be repeated. So the six-note picking pattern on each beat is: down–down–down–up–*pull-off*–up.

TRACK 43

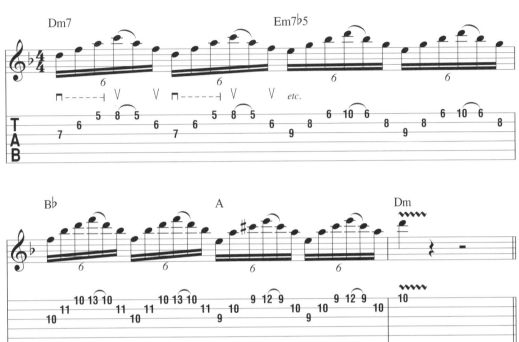

Although it's not nearly as common, you can flip this idea on its head and use descending sweeps, as well. Here's an idea to demonstrate that. Notice that the arrangement of notes on each string and the picking pattern are the exact opposite of that in Track 43.

TRACK 44

Extended Sweeping

When you carry the sweeps further, you get the extended sweeps, which can be extended all the way through all six strings if you'd like. The overwhelmingly common use for this idea is triad arpeggios played at blazing speed, but other interesting sounds are ripe for the picking as well, if you care to explore. Before we do that, though, let's check out this technique's bread and butter: Fast and furious arpeggios.

Here's a classic application: The two-octave minor arpeggio based off string 5. In 12th position, it's in A minor. We employ a hammer-on on the bottom and a pull-off at the top in order to keep the picking unidirectional. Aside from the picking, the other challenge for this lick is maintaining cleanliness in the fret hand, particularly during the rolling maneuver on strings 4 and 3. You want to avoid having any two notes ring together. It's not terribly difficult when ascending, but when you're descending, if you don't position your ring finger just right, it's very easy to accidently nudge string 2 on fret 14, which will produce an ugly C♯ note. So, for this one, as with all of these sweeping licks, be extra sure that your fret hand is clean before you speed things up.

 TRACK 45

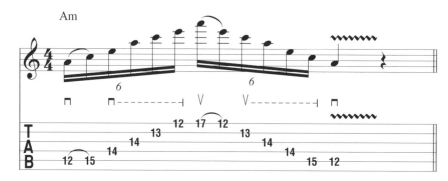

If you stretch a bit on string 5 instead of string 1, you can replace the note A with G and turn this shape into a C major arpeggio with a low G (the 5th) in the bass.

 TRACK 46

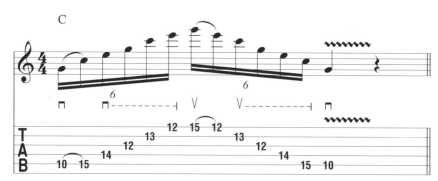

The major version with the root on string 5 as the lowest note is even more trying on the fret hand, as it requires you to roll your finger (most people use their middle finger) across three adjacent strings. Following is an example in 10th position for a G major arpeggio. Again, be sure to practice this very slowly before bringing it up to speed.

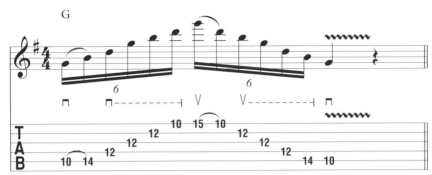

Summary

Economy picking feels strange the first time you try it, and many players shy away from it for that very fact; they figure they've already learned how to alternate pick for so many years that it's too late in the game to learn something new. I would encourage you to rethink that idea. Economy picking opens a whole new door of technical possibilities and sounds that would be very difficult with alternate picking. One method is not better than the other, and they both have their uses, but being fluent in both will only make you a more versatile player. Again, the main hurdles that face beginning economy pickers are:

- **Lopsided rhythms:** It will take a bit of time to gain control over your timing if you're new to this method. This is perfectly normal and doesn't mean that you're simply "not cut out for it" or anything. With slow, steady practice, you'll most likely start to feel comfortable within a week or so.

- **Pick orientation:** You may need to adjust your pick angle/slant, depending on which direction you're moving (ascending or descending). Again, this is normal, and you can clearly see players like Gambale do this when they play. It makes perfect sense when you think about it. Since every player's hands are slightly different, you'll need to experiment to find which movements make it easiest for you.

- **Clarity:** This mainly applies to extended sweeping. Many times when inexperienced players sweep arpeggios, everything, aside from the top and bottom notes, kind of just sounds like mush. You want your arpeggios to have the same clarity as your scalar lines, and that requires a careful choreography of your two hands. The picking motion (the sweep) needs to be timed correctly and your fret-hand fingers should press down only at the appropriate time. If you hold several notes down at once, like a chord, everything will ring together and sound like mush.

Applied Techniques

Our first economy example uses the A Mixolydian mode (save for one bluesy, chromatic C♮ note) and uses the Eric Johnson/Yngwie Malmsteen-approved method of only sweeping through strings when using a downstroke. After the pickup phrase and initial ascent, we get into a pattern on strings 2 and 1: downstroke on string 2, (continued) downstroke on string 1, upstroke on string 1, and pull-off. This four-note sequence is played at three different pitch levels before the lick concludes.

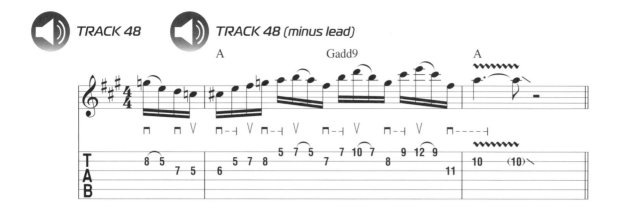

This next lick is in C minor and fully exploits the economy technique, sweeping on both down- and upstrokes. After an introductory phrase in measure 1, the picking choreography begins in measure 2 with the same two-notes-per-string idea we saw in Tracks 38 and 39. Notice that, on beats 2–3, we're descending the C minor pentatonic scale, but we've arranged it with the G note on string 3, fret 12 (instead of string 2, fret 8) to facilitate the economy technique.

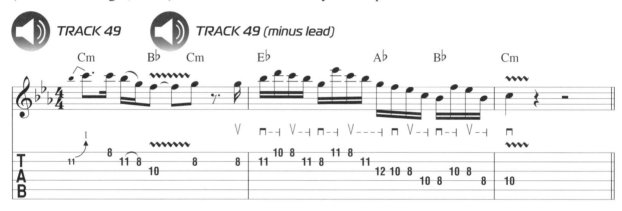

In the style of shredmaster Yngwie Malmsteen, this example demonstrates how this technique is perfectly suited for playing diminished arpeggios. Experiment with the picking on beat 1 in measure 3 to see what feels best. You may prefer alternate picking or a version of economy picking. For the diminished arpeggios, however, we'll pick them just the way Yngwie does.

Here's another take on the sweeping technique—something in the vein of Steve Vai. We're sweeping extended harmonies here instead of triad arpeggios. The first measure is pretty straightforward, but work through the second measure carefully to make sure that you're getting the picking and rhythms right. Even though it's just straight 16th notes, the interspersed slides and pull-offs provide several opportunities for rushing if you're not careful.

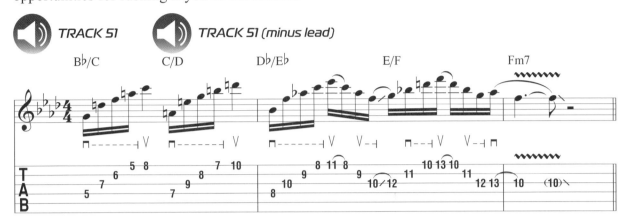

In this lick, we're again working on the top three strings exclusively—very common sweeping territory. This one works up through various inversions of Dm7 and Dm9 arpeggios, culminating in the high D tonic note at fret 22. Watch the rhythm carefully in this one, as we slow down from 16th-note triplets in measure 1 to standard 16th notes at the beginning of measure 2 before finishing off with another 16th-note triplet. Similar to the diminished arpeggios of Track 50, we're only using downward sweeps here.

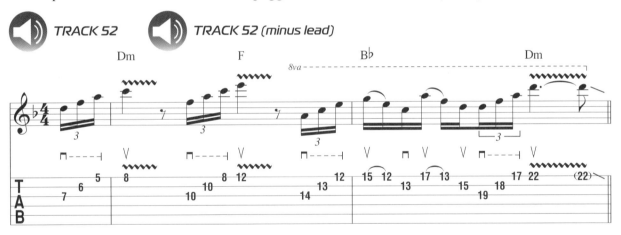

We'll close out with a sweeping tour de force, including five-string sweeps alternated with two-string mini-sweeps. Pay close attention to the picking, making sure that you're taking full advantage of the sweeping motion. This one's not easy (for me anyway!), so work it up carefully.

The exercises in this chapter are designed to help you master the uses of hammer-ons, pull-offs, and slides. Although this technique is especially attractive to beginners because of the speed that can be obtained, it should be noted that legato playing can become a crutch. It's important not to neglect the picking techniques, as the smooth sound of legato will most likely not be applicable to every musical situation.

By the same token, it's a common misconception that legato playing is "easier" than picking. Many people often assume that if they can play a lick by picking every note, then they can surely do the same with an all-legato approach. This is definitely not the case. Both techniques require diligent practice to master, as they draw upon different muscle groups, types of coordination, etc.

Tracks 54 and 55 are exactly the same as Tracks 2 and 3, except here they are performed entirely with hammer-ons and pull-offs. If you've never done this before, you'll realize very quickly that the "if you can pick it, you can play it legato" notion is certainly false. These exercises are a serious workout for your fret hand, so take breaks when you need them.

Be sure that all the notes are clean and audible, especially when pulling off. In the latter case, many players find it helpful to prepare for the pulled-off notes by planting all fingers at once, then beginning the pull-off(s). Another key issue to watch is timing. Make sure that nothing sounds lopsided and that each note is given equal time. Again, if you've never worked on this type of exercise before, don't get frustrated—it's not easy!

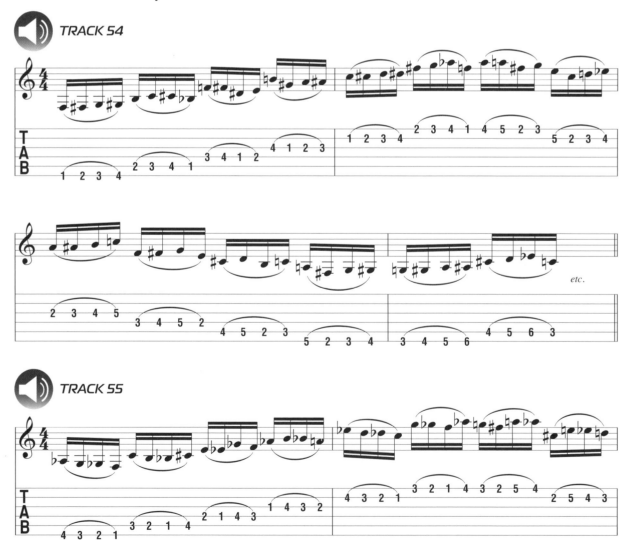

TRACK 54

TRACK 55

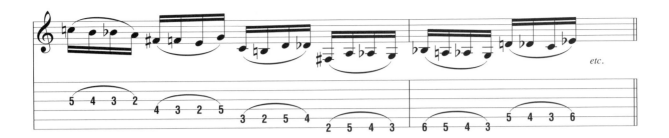

etc.

A Game of Millimeters

Legato playing requires great fret-hand stamina. If you're not used to this kind of thing—with all four fingers working hard—your forearm is going to start to burn pretty quickly. It only makes sense that, the less you move, the less you'll tax your muscles. Therefore, try to minimize your movement as much as possible. Watch your fret-hand technique closely to see if one or more of your fingers is needlessly flailing away from the fretboard at any time. Usually, this is simply a byproduct of not paying attention to this unintended motion. The good news is that these kinds of habits can often be eliminated by simply becoming aware of it and making a conscious effort to change it.

This next exercise is kind of a fun way to work on specific finger combinations: 1/3 and 2/4. Be sure that you're using the indicated fret-hand fingering; otherwise, you defeat the purpose of the exercise.

TRACK 56

This example applies legato technique to a melodic sequence in C major performed entirely on the top two strings. You'll get practice with several different finger combinations here if you follow the indicated fingering.

 TRACK 57

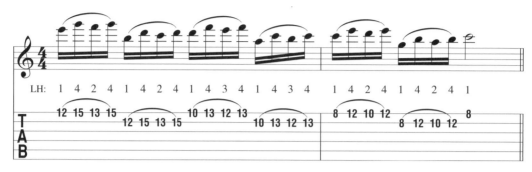

Here's a nice ascending lick in A major that applies a similar 16th-note sequence to two different starting pitches: first A, and then D. In measure 2, the same exact thing is repeated up an octave. This means that we have a quick little shift from fourth position to sixth position. Although your index, middle, and pinky see most of the action here, on beat 4 of each measure, we have the pinky and ring finger working in tandem, which is generally the most troublesome combination for most people. Make sure that the notes are clearly audible in those spots and played in proper rhythm.

 TRACK 58

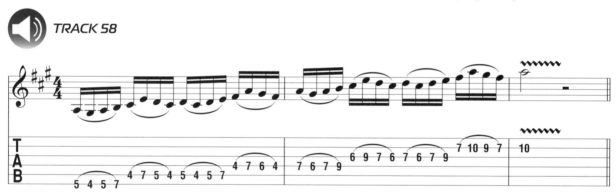

"Hammer-Ons from Nowhere"

If you've watched Steve Vai much, you've no doubt seen him stop picking completely (often, he grabs the body of the guitar with the pick hand and lifts it up) and play legato barrages exclusively with the fret hand. How does he do this? It's a technique that's sometimes called the *hammer-on from nowhere*. Despite its mysterious name, chances are, you've already done it—at least by accident.

The idea is that, when descending scalar licks, you don't *have* to pick the note on a lower string when moving to it. The technique is easier to show than it is to describe, so I'll do that.

For example, instead of playing this:

 *TRACK 59*

You can do this:

 *TRACK 60*

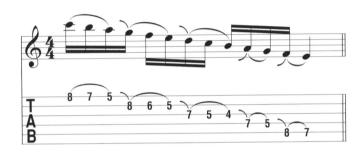

In the second example, you're only picking once—the very first note of the lick.

What's going on here? Every time you see the little half slur (i.e., before the first note on strings 2–5), it indicates that the "hammer-on from nowhere" should be used. You simply hammer onto the string instead of picking it. If you're using a typical distorted rock tone, the note should speak loud and clear, assuming you execute a solid hammer. It sounds ultra-slippery this way, and it makes it harder to tell when you're changing strings.

Gettin' Down

I mentioned earlier that the hammer-from-nowhere technique is used on descending licks, which is most often the case. Why? Well, it's just a logistical issue. Think about it: If you end with your index finger on string 3, for example, and then you hammer onto string 4 with your middle, ring, or pinky, you're most likely going to mute string 3 while you do that (unless, of course, you've got your fingers super-arched, as in classical guitar). The hammer-from-nowhere makes it easy to get a clean note.

Now take the opposite approach. Let's say you end with your pinky on string 4 and you want to hammer string 3 with your index. It's certainly not impossible, but it requires you to perfectly time the release of your pinky just before you hammer with your index. It also requires you to mute string 4 immediately afterward. This can be accomplished with the tip of your index finger or with the pick-hand palm. It's not impossible by any means, but it's certainly not as easy as the descending version. To see what I mean, try playing Track 60 backwards—from last note to first—while only picking the first note.

Here's a lengthy legato sequence in F major that makes use of this technique. After picking the first note, you won't need your pick again until the D note on the "and" of beat 4 of measure 2. Notice that the sequence changes on string 6, so keep an eye out. You'll also be working on legato slides here.

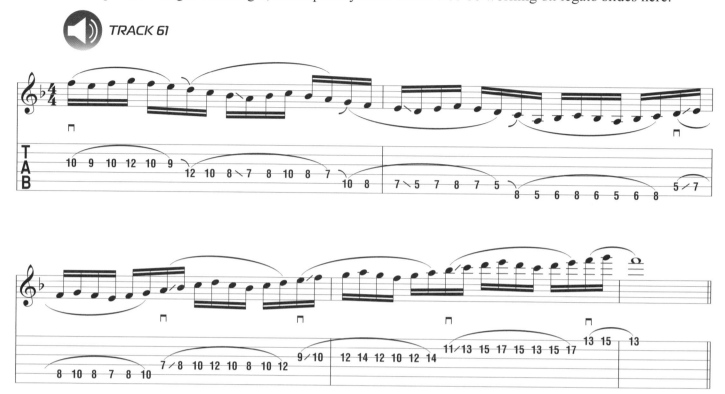

TRACK 61

Summary

Legato technique is a completely different animal than picking, and it needs to be practiced with the same diligence if you want to master it. The idea that "if you can pick it, you can play it with legato" is completely false—unless, of course, you've practiced playing legato a whole bunch! Legato masters like Joe Satriani, Steve Vai, and Allan Holdsworth have dedicated years of practice to developing their style, and there's no shortcut. If you want to play legato like a master, you have to put the time in.

Legato requires another kind of physical stamina and uses different muscles than when picking exclusively. Like I said, when you first start working on the 1–2–3–4 exercises at the beginning of this chapter, your forearm will likely get very sore, very quickly. But the strength will come with practice, just as with anything else. Try to keep the following in mind with regard to your legato playing:

- **Minimize movement:** Try to find the smallest movement necessary for each maneuver. For example, with a hammer-on, you need to lift the hammering finger up a bit in order to execute the hammer, but experiment to find out exactly how high you need to lift it in order to produce a solid hammered note. With pull-offs, experiment with how far down and how quickly you need to pull off in order to produce a clear note. Not only will this make you more efficient, but careful attention to detail like this will only help make you a cleaner player.

- **Work all the fingers:** The pinky is notoriously underused by guitar players, but it's specifically the combination of the pinky and ring finger that's the real issue. This is the weakest fingering pair of all (trilling between every possible pair of fingers will clearly make this evident). Nevertheless, it needs to be included in the reindeer games if you expect to be able to use it in your solos. So, be sure to work it into your practice routine regularly to make sure that it's in good shape.

- **Legato can be a problem-solver:** Legato isn't only about the sound; it can also ease the burden on your picking hand at times. Sure, if you want to be stubborn, you can beat your head against the wall until you're able to pick *every* single note of that crazy lick. Or you can just accept the fact that adding a hammer-on or pull-off here and there can make it much easier and will most likely sound just as cool. I often prefer the sound of mixing legato and picking together, and that's probably the technique I end up using the most when I'm actually playing music.

Applied Techniques

Here's a metal-approved legato excursion in E minor that demonstrates a typical application of the legato technique. The first measure, if performed with the index, ring, and pinky, serves as an excellent workout for the third and fourth fingers. Pay close attention to the end of each positional group, as the sequence of notes is altered slightly to prepare for the shift. Regarding the picking hand, I find this lick to be a good place to employ economy picking (i.e., one continuous upstroke from string 1 to string 2 at the beginning of each beat).

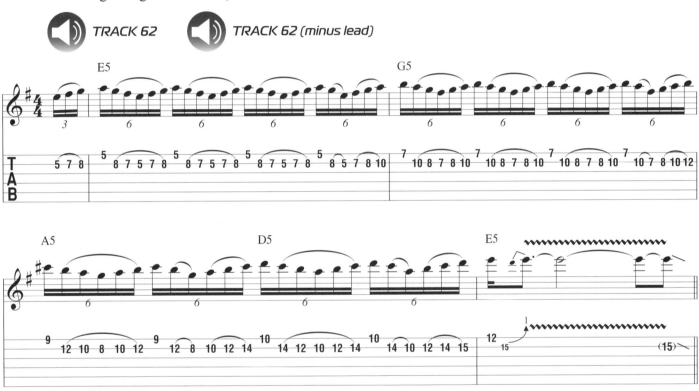

This lick applies the technique in a string-crossing pentatonic fashion. Even blues players such as Stevie Ray Vaughan have used this type of trick occasionally. Of course, he would do so with a much less distorted tone, so it sounded slightly different. Notice the use of several hammers-from-nowhere.

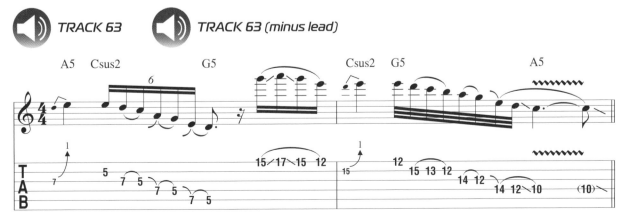

Here's a barn-burner in A minor that makes use of some stretches in the fret hand. At this spot on the neck, they're not too painful, however. The pick is used minimally here in favor of hammers-from-nowhere, which are employed whenever possible.

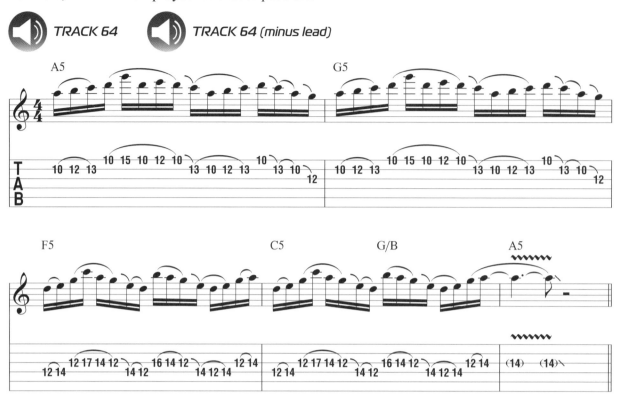

Finally, here's a D Dorian lick that's based mostly in 10th position, although it does shift to ninth position for the second half of measure 1. I've included my picking preference here so you can see how economy picking can be exploited to increase speed during these types of licks. I've mixed in a few hammers-from-nowhere, but specifically did not use the technique at every opportunity. This helps give the lick a slightly more aggressive tone, which is what I wanted for this one.

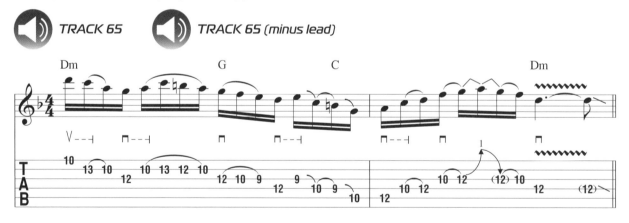

AFTERWORD

Well, that wraps it up. Hopefully, you've enjoyed the examples in this book and will continue to work on them to improve your technique. Proficiency on an instrument is not a short-term endeavor; it takes lots of work to attain world-class chops. And, once you get there, you can't exactly rest on your laurels. If you don't use it, you lose it, as they say. So be prepared to seek out new licks, songs, styles, etc. to keep you inspired and motivated to practice. Fortunately, with the wealth of musical expression available to us in this day and age, this shouldn't be a problem. In this regard, looking to different instruments (piano, violin, sax, etc.) is often eye-opening, as the licks idiomatic to them will often be quite different than those normally played on guitar.

Best of luck to you in your musical adventures, and remember: Patience paired with discipline will yield rewarding results. Break a leg!

The following scales and arpeggios are some of the most common in rock and popular music. Each is shown in root position, spanning two octaves.

Note: This is intended as a reference. Some scale and arpeggio types (e.g., major, minor, pentatonic, blues) are much more heavily used than others, and those that the reader finds most useful should be practiced in multiple positions across the fretboard and in different keys.

Scales

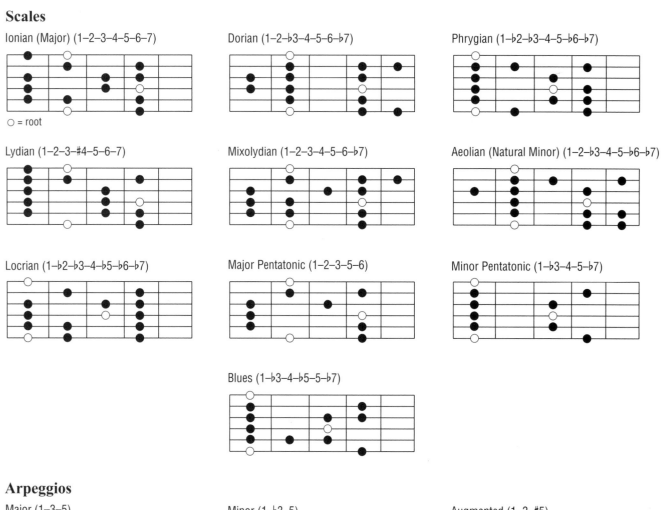

Arpeggios

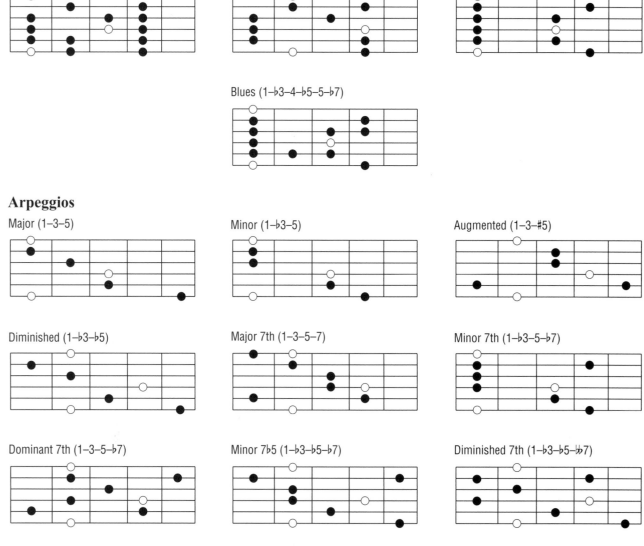